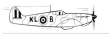

# THE PAST *in pictures*

# The Home Front

*Fiona Reynoldson*

WAYLAND

# THE PAST *in pictures*

## *Titles in this series* ✷ The Victorians ✷ The Home Front

Editor: Elizabeth Gogerly
Original Design: Roger Hammond/Joyce Chester
Design: Joyce Chester

First published in 1999 by Wayland Publishers Limited, 61
Western Road, Hove, East Sussex BN3 1JD

Find Wayland on the Internet at http://www.wayland.co.uk

**British Library Cataloguing in Publication Data**

Reynoldson, Fiona
The Home Front. – (The past in pictures)
1. Great Britain – Social conditions – 20th century –
Pictorial works – Juvenile literature
I. Title
941' 084

ISBN 07502 2372 3

Typeset by Joyce Chester
Printed and bound in Italy by G. Canale & C. S.p.A., Turin

**Picture Acknowledgements**
· The publishers would like to thank the following for permission to
reproduce their pictures:
AKG 17 (middle, right); The Beamish North of England Open Air
Museum 28 (bottom), 44 (far right); Bridgeman/Imperial War Museum
15 (top); Dennis Day *cover* (background); E.T Archive 4 (left), 17 (top,
left), 19 (bottom); Mary Evans 17 (bottom), 33 (middle, left); John
Frost 25 (top); Getty 13 (middle, left), 25 (bottom), 27 (left), 31 (top,
left); Robin Holyoake 25 (top); Imperial War Museum 4 (right), 5
(bottom, left), 7 (middle, left), 8 (bottom), 9 (bottom & middle, right),
11 (top & right), 12, 14, 15 (bottom), 16 (top & bottom), 18 (bottom,
left), 19 (top), 20 (left & right), 21 (top & bottom), 22 (top), 23 (top,
left), 24 (bottom), 25 (middle & bottom), 29 (middle & bottom), 30
(bottom), 32 (bottom), 33 (top), 34 (bottom), 35 (top), 36 top &
bottom), 37 (top), 38 (botttom), 39 (bottom), 42, 43 (top, right) 45
*(cover,* third right), 45 *(cover,* second left) Peter Newark Military
Pictures *cover* (Winston Churchill); Robert Opie 7 (bottom), 13
(bottom, right), 22 (bottom, left), 23 (bottom, left), 26 (middle, right),
27 (bottom, right), 31 (top, right), 32 (top, right), 41(top, left), 43
(middle, left); Popperfoto 5 (bottom, right), 10, 13 (top), 22 (top), 26
(left), 31(bottom, right), 35 (bottom, right), 37 (bottom, left), 40 (top &
bottom), 41 (bottom, right), 43 (bottom, left); Public Record Office 7
(top, right), 24 (top, right), 27 (top, right), 28 (top, right), 30 (top, right),
35 (bottom, left), 37 (middle, left); Fiona Reynoldson 15 (middle);
Science and Society 5 (top), 6 (middle), 9 (top), 29 (top), 34 (top);
Scottish Highland Photo Library 39 (top); © Topham 23 (middle);
Wayland 6 (left), 8 (top), 18 (top), 21 (middle)/ © Aberdeen Journals 38
(top)/ © Press Journal 33 (bottom, left).

# The Home Front

## Contents

# War Is Coming

Adolf Hitler was the German leader in the 1930s. He promised to make Germany powerful by building up the army and the airforce and by taking land from neighbouring countries. Other European countries worried that war might come soon.

▼ Adolf Hitler addressing a rally in Germany. He wanted to lead Germany to greatness again and because he was such a brilliant speaker, German people listened to him willingly.

▲ German propaganda posters show Hitler and his political party, the National Socialists (Nazis), as a strong military force. In this poster you can also see the swastika, which was the symbol for Nazi Germany.

◄ By the mid 1930s Britain was building up the RAF (Royal Air Force). New aeroplanes were developed such as the famous Spitfire fighter plane.

▼ By the end of the 1930s, Germany was taking land from other countries around her. When Hitler sent German forces into Poland, Britain and France decided they had given Germany enough warnings, and on 3rd September 1939, Britain declared war on Germany. The Second World War had begun.

**NEWS** OF THE **WORLD** **WAR DECLARED** (OFFICIAL)

► In 1937 King George VI became king. His wife was called Elizabeth. George VI and Elizabeth were king and queen throughout the war. They had two daughters called Princess Elizabeth (now Queen Elizabeth II) and Margaret.

GOD BLESS OUR KING AND QUEEN

CANADA INDIA AUSTRALIA NEW ZEA

Souvenir of the CORONATION 12th May 1937.

**H.M. KING GEORGE VI.**
Born 14th Dec., 1895. Created Duke of York 1920. Married 26th April, 1923, Lady Elizabeth Bowes-Lyon, and has two daughters: H. R. H. Princess Elizabeth, born 21st April, 1926; and H. R. H. Princess Margaret Rose, born 21st August, 1930. Succeeded (on the abdication of his elder brother, Edward VIII), 11th Dec., 1936.

# Gas Attack

Gas was a deadly new weapon. It had been used during the First World War and many soldiers had been killed. If gas was dropped from aeroplanes it could kill or injure many people. The government decided to give everyone a gas mask to wear if there was a gas attack.

▼ These people are practising in case of gas attack. Gas cannot be seen so the tops of pillar boxes were painted with special yellow paint that would change colour if there was gas in the air.

◄ Gas masks had to be carried at all times in their cardboard box which had a long strap of string. Many cinemas and restaurants would not let people in without their gas masks.

Gas masks for adults and children had filters in the 'nose' so that a person kept the gas mask on but could breathe through the filter. However, babies were completely enclosed inside their masks so someone had to pump air into the mask all the time so the baby could breathe.

OFFICIAL INSTRUCTIONS ISSUED BY THE MINISTRY OF HOME SECURITY

# GAS ATTACK

## HOW TO PUT ON YOUR GAS MASK

Always keep your gas mask with you — day and night. Learn to put it on quickly. Practise wearing it.

1. Hold your breath.
2. Hold mask in front of face, with thumbs inside straps.
3. Thrust chin well forward into mask, pull straps over head as far as they will go.
4. Run finger round face-piece taking care headstraps are not twisted.

## IF THE GAS RATTLES SOUND

1. Hold your breath. Put on mask, wherever you are. Close window.

2. If out of doors, take off hat, put on your mask. Turn up collar.

3. Put on gloves or keep hands in pockets. Take cover in nearest building.

## YOU GET GASSED

Keep your gas mask on even if you feel discomfort. If discomfort continues go to First Aid Post

| | 2 | 3 | 4 |
|---|---|---|---|
| ...but *don't* ...the splash ...handker... ...Then ...y hand... | Rub No. 2 Ointment well into place. *(Buy a 6d. jar now from any chemist).* In emergency chemists supply Bleach Cream free. | If you can't get Ointment or Cream within 5 minutes wash place with soap and warm water | Take off at once any garment splashed with gas. |

▲ The government gave out lots of leaflets on what to do if there was a gas attack.

► Throughout the war the British sense of humour kept people going. This cartoon shows how even the threat of gas attack had its funny side.

"We had Harricot beans for dinner to-day!"

# Evacuation

At the start of the war the government knew that cities would be bombed. They decided to send all the children from the cities to the country where they would be safe. About three million children left their homes and went to the country.

> " We didn't lose one single child or have one accident. "
>
> HUGH ELLER, LONDON COUNTY COUNCIL EVACUATION AREA ORGANIZER

▼ Children at the railway station. Every child had a label with his or her name on because some of the children were as young as five years old. They carried all their things to the big railway stations where trains waited to take them to the country.

▲ Parents were given lists of what to pack in a knapsack or carrier bag. This included some clothes, a day's food to eat while travelling and, of course, a gas mask.

► After many hours on the train, the children arrived in the country. The children were tired and confused. It was the end of a long day.

▼ City children learnt about country life and some children worked on the farms. By Christmas 1939, no bombs had fallen and many children returned to the cities.

▼ The government wanted children to stay away from the cities and the bombs. This poster shows that mothers who brought their children back from the countryside were just doing what Hitler wanted.

TAKE THEM BACK!
TAKE THEM BACK!
TAKE THEM BACK!..

DON'T do it, Mother —
LEAVE THE CHILDREN WHERE THEY ARE

# The Invasion Threat

By May 1940, most children were back home in the cities. No bombs had fallen so people called it the Phoney War. However, what was real was that Germany swept into France and drove British and French forces back to the coast at a place called Dunkirk.

66 Our troops were retreating from Dunkirk and we were getting them back as best we could. Anyone who owned a boat was asked to volunteer to go over there and help. 99

**DONALD McMORRAN**
DORKING, SURREY

◄ The British soldiers waited on the beaches at Dunkirk to be picked up. Every day the Germans were getting closer and their bombers were overhead. Boats arrived from England to pick them up. The soldiers waded into the water leaving the tanks and guns behind as they clambered into boats. This soldier has been rescued.

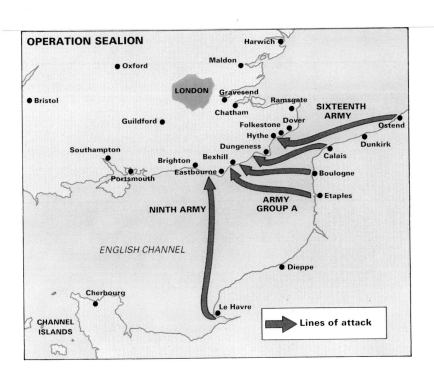

OPERATION SEALION

◄ With the British army driven from France and the French defeated, the Germans wanted to invade Britain in the summer of 1940. The plan was known as Operation Sealion. You can see from this map how threatened the British people felt.

► The government decided to have all the signposts taken down. That way the Germans would have to find out for themselves which road led to London. Road blocks were put on main roads from the South Coast to London.

".... *strictly between these four walls!*"

CARELESS TALK COSTS LIVES

◄ The government also worried about spies. Artists designed posters telling people not to talk in public about anything that might help the enemy. People were told to be wary at all times in case a spy was listening to their conversations.

# The Home Guard

Thousands of young men were needed to become soldiers but there were also many men who were older who could do jobs that were important to the war. The government asked for men between the ages of seventeen and sixty-five to come forward and be trained to fight if Britain was invaded.

▼ Home Guards often joined up in groups. There were groups of taxi drivers, railway workers, even 17-year-old schoolboys from Eton. To start with the Home Guard were called the Local Defence Volunteers (LDV) and they practised in their own clothes and drilled with old guns or even wooden guns.

> 66 On patrol one night we saw a great white cloud sitting on the marsh. We decided it must be a German parachutist. We ran forward, guns at the ready. We couldn't see the paratrooper and we began to dig at the parachute to get it out. Then, to our horror we saw it was attached to a bomb! We snatched up our guns and ran. 99
>
> **WILFRID GRAY,** HOME GUARD

▲ By 1943 there were two million men in the Home Guard. Although the threat of invasion wasn't as great as in the early days of the war, the Home Guard still had to train. They now had uniforms and proper guns, they manned anti-aircraft guns and trained in bomb disposal.

► The Home Guard was a way of life for many men for nearly five years. It had also been a great source of comradeship and humour as this book of jokes shows.

▲ A few women also wanted to train to fight in case of invasion. Mrs Randall of Slough started a Women's Fighting Service, trained by the Home Guard.

HOME GUARD *Humour* 1/6 DURING FOUR AND A HALF YEARS

# Battle of Britain

To invade Britain Hitler knew he must shoot down the RAF. This massive air battle became known as the Battle of Britain. The RAF fought the German planes daily but after three months, the British were running out of aeroplanes and trained pilots. The Germans were giving up too and decided to stop attacking the airfields and bomb the cities instead.

▼ Pilots running to their aeroplanes. When news came in that German planes were approaching Britain, the pilots were 'scrambled'. This meant that they grabbed their parachutes and helmets and ran to their planes so they could take off and meet the German planes in the sky.

► Aeroplanes fighting over the south coast of England. The most famous German fighter plane was the Messerschmitt 109. The most famous British fighter planes were the Spitfire and the Hurricane.

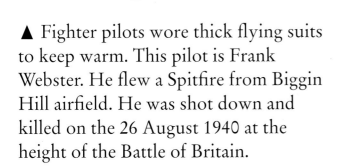

▼ Children sheltering in a trench in a Kentish hopfield, watching an air battle.

> 66 Never in the field of human conflict, has so much been owed by so many to so few. 99
>
> **WINSTON CHURCHILL**

▲ Fighter pilots wore thick flying suits to keep warm. This pilot is Frank Webster. He flew a Spitfire from Biggin Hill airfield. He was shot down and killed on the 26 August 1940 at the height of the Battle of Britain.

# The Blitz

The British gave the name the Blitz to the German bombing of British cities. The Germans wanted to destroy factories and railways and also to frighten the British into surrendering, so they bombed cities like Glasgow, Coventry Portsmouth and London.

▲ A little girl being rescued from a bombed house by an Air Raid Warden.

◄ Whole streets could be devastated by a bomb blast. Here the prime minister, Winston Churchill, looks at the damage in a badly bombed residential area.

◄ During the height of the Blitz, London was bombed 75 nights out of 76. The fires started by the bombs were so bad that people were afraid that they would get out of control. And on one very bad night the Thames was so low it was difficult to get enough water to fight the fires.

66 I looked up and it was the most amazing sight. There were hundreds of German bombers making the sky dark. There was a roar of engines, an explosion of bombs. I wasn't afraid. There was too much danger to be afraid. 99

A FIFTEEN YEAR OLD BOY WATCHING FROM THE NORTH DOWNS IN SURREY

'ARF A MO'

NATIONAL SERVICE NEEDS YOU

*LEARN NOW! – BE READY!*

▲ A bus in a bomb crater.

◄ A poster encouraging people to join up and work with the fire service.

# The Blackout

Cities are a mass of light at night so it was easy to see them from aeroplanes. No one wanted the German pilots to see any lights in the houses and streets below them so there were strict rules. This was called the Blackout. Houses had to have special curtains because ordinary curtains showed light.

▼ There were many accidents because people could not see where they were going in the Blackout. At first cars were not allowed headlights but there were so many road accidents that eventually some light was allowed. Even then the beams of light always had to point downwards.

CYCLE LAMP BLACK OUT SET.

● ● ●

One Black Mask with 1¼ inch Red Centre, to convert an ordinary front lamp into a Rear Lamp.

One front lamp Dimming Mask Black with White Bottom.

These Masks meet Regulation requirements.

▲ In the Blackout torches had to be pointed towards the ground but even the torch light was supposed to be covered with tissue paper. Cycle head lamps were covered with special covers, as were car headlights, and even traffic lights were covered so just a small cross of light showed through.

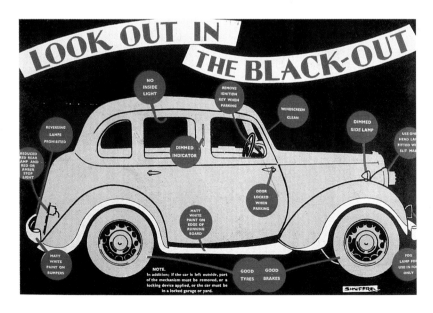

LOOK OUT IN THE BLACK-OUT

► Many animals were hit by cars in the dark so some farmers painted their cows with white stripes. Edges of pavements and lamp-posts were also painted with white stripes.

▼ Big railway stations had to be blacked out. Just a few lights were allowed under the cover of the roof so that people could read timetables.

66 It was inky black and I had no torch so I could not see where the canal was as I walked home. I groped along by the bushes but I was frankly terrified and in the end I went down on hands and knees and crawled all the way home. I met two people crawling the other way. 99

A MAN LIVING IN MANCHESTER

# Taking Shelter

Despite the Blackout, the anti-aircraft guns and the RAF, many bombs fell on the cities. At the beginning of the war these were bombs dropped from aeroplanes but towards the end the Germans had invented two new weapons. These were called the V1 and V2. People needed to shelter from all this bombing.

▼ Anderson shelters were made of steel. Once you received one you had to dig a deep hole in your garden and half bury the shelter with soil. Some people made the shelters look more attractive by growing flowers over them, while others grew much needed vegetables.

▲ Lots of people slept in these shelters every night during the Blitz. Many of those people owed their lives to their shelters. These two women have woken up to find their house demolished.

> 66 My mother was still scrambling under the table when I saw the walls of the room crumbling and tumbling towards us. An electric fire bounced across the room. I saw my father holding on to the cooker and go up in the air and down again. I don't remember any sounds but suddenly all I could see was the night sky. Our house had completely vanished. 99
>
> **GERALD COLE,** LONDON

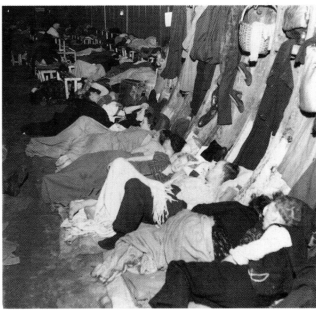

▲ Every night thousands of Londoners took their bedding and went down the Underground to sleep. This was the only place where you could not hear the bombs and in the morning people got up and went off to work. Children were often sent early in the evening to find a space and save it for the adults later.

▲ An Air Raid Warden's helmet and rattle. There were Air Raid Wardens for every area. Their job was to warn people if an air raid was due. They went down the streets with the rattle and often shouting as well. They organized the rescue services when there was a bombing raid.

► A Morrison shelter. These were heavy, metal tables with wire sides that people could use inside their homes as dining tables or even for table tennis.

# Rationing

Rationing began early in the war. A lot of Britain's food came from other countries in ships. Once the war started German submarines attacked ships bringing food to Britain. This meant that there was less food to go round. Rationing made sure there was enough food for everybody to survive.

▼ Picture of a week's rations for one person. Some foods were not rationed but might be impossible to get hold of. Things that came from foreign countries, such as coffee and oranges, were either rationed or rare.

▲ Everyone had a ration book which contained coupons for food. Rationing was fair. It did not matter how much money you had you could not get more than your share because you had to give in one of the coupons as well as money when you went shopping. Every person had to register with a particular shop for all their groceries.

> 66 Everyone talks about food. An astonishing amount of people's time is occupied by discussing ways and means of making rations go further. 99
>
> MOLLIE PANTER-DOWNES
> JUNE 1, 1941

◀ A poster about saving food. The government set up a Ministry of Food. Everyone was told not to waste food.

▼ Most of the shopping and cooking was done by women. They had to work out nourishing meals with very little food. Sometimes they heard that something special had arrived such as a load of fish or some oranges. Everyone rushed out to the shop. Often they queued for hours.

◀ Here is a selection of the kinds of foods sometimes available in the shops. Dried eggs were used in place of fresh eggs which had become rationed.

# Dig for Victory

Despite rationing, Britain needed more food. Farmers, as well as ordinary people, were asked to grow more crops and vegetables. Most people were keen and dug up their lawns to grow carrots, leeks and potatoes.

► A poster encouraging people to grow more vegetables. The government made lots of posters to encourage people to grow more food, particularly vegetables such as potatoes and carrots which are filling and grow easily in Britain.

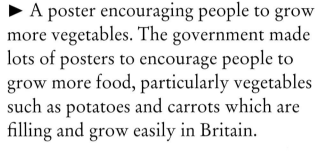

66 I promise as my Christmas gift to sailors who have to bring our bread that I will do all I can to eat home grown potatoes. 99

A PROMISE VISITORS WERE ASKED TO SIGN, CHRISTMAS POTATO FAIR IN 1942

◄ Pigs were popular because everyone loved bacon and ham. Neighbours formed pig clubs. They shared the cost of buying a pig and then they shared looking after it. Everyone saved scraps to feed the pig and pig bins were put in the street for people to put left overs in. When the pig was old enough to be killed, the meat was shared out.

► There were many wartime recipe books especially written to help people make the most of the food available. Housewives were told how to use home grown vegetables. Hot beetroot in a white sauce with roast potatoes, for example, was a good hearty meal without using up a meat ration.

▲ Nurses at Guy's Hospital in London grew vegetables for the hospital kitchen after part of the hospital was bombed.

► People grew vegetables wherever they could. Many people had allotments but lawns, railway embankments, public parks and even bomb sites were turned into vegetable gardens.

# Clothes Rationing

Clothes were rationed too. People were given sixty-six coupons a year for new clothes. Every time a person bought shoes or any item of clothing they had to give some coupons as well as pay money. Seven coupons could be exchanged for a dress and eight coupons for trousers.

▶ People were encouraged to make as many clothes for themselves as possible. Patterns for clothes were designed to cut down on material and were often made without pockets. Turn-ups were left off trousers and skirts were shorter.

◀ Clothes were designed that were sensible and neat and would not use very much material. Some of these clothes were called Utility clothes and had a special label on them.

► Clever mothers made clothes from adult cast-offs. A child's coat could be made from a woman's full skirt or even a man's old coat. The government issued posters like these to encourage people to make the most of their old clothes.

**MAKE DO AND MEND**

> 66 Mend and make do to avoid buying new. 99
>
> A GOVERNMENT SLOGAN

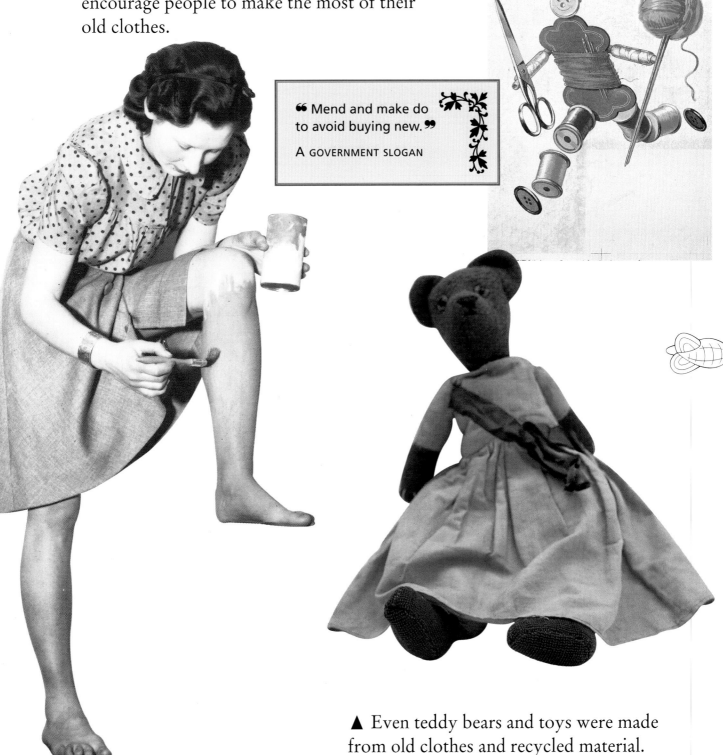

▲ Even teddy bears and toys were made from old clothes and recycled material.

# Save and Salvage

During the war the government asked people to save all kinds of things they might normally throw away. The most valuable thing was aluminium. People were told that if everyone saved the aluminium tops on milk bottles then fifty bombers could be built each year. Salvaging 'rubbish' made everyone feel they were a part of the war effort.

▲ Government posters encouraged everyone to save and recycle aluminium, paper, old clothes and iron. The iron could be from old bicycles, bedsteads or even garden railings and gates. Unfortunately, a great deal of the metal collected was not much use for building planes.

▼ Children were very good collectors. They were keen and energetic. The government formed a special club called Cogs which children joined through school. In some places Cogs doubled the amount of rubbish collected.

► People were also asked to save paper. Fifty-six million books were collected and pulped down to make recycled paper. These boys have collected a boxful of old newspapers.

▼ This government poster encouraged people to buy war savings bonds. This was a way of lending money to the government so that it could buy guns, tanks, ships, and aeroplanes.

66 Women of Britain, give us your aluminium pots and pans. We will turn them into Spitfires, Hurricanes, Blenheims and Wellingtons. 99

**LORD BEAVERBROOK**, JULY 1940

► Schools and sometimes whole villages, worked to raise money to buy guns or even aeroplanes. They raised the money in many ways, from selling war bonds or certificates to having bazaars.

# Pulling Together

Many terrible things happened during the war. Servicemen were killed fighting all over the world. At home families were bombed and killed or made homeless. Though nobody starved, food was boring. Clothes were in short supply and life could be quite dull. Yet many people look back on the war as a time when everyone pulled together for one thing – victory over the enemy.

"We shall not fail, and then some day, when children ask: What did you do to win this inheritance for us and to make our name so respected among men?" one will say: "I was a Fighter Pilot," another will say: "I was in the Submarine Service," another: "I marched with the Eighth Army," a fourth will say:"None of you could have lived without the convoys and the Merchant Seamen," and *you*, in *your* turn will say, with equal pride and with equal right: "WE CUT THE COAL."

Winston Churchill
OCTOBER 31st, 1942

▲ Winston Churchill became prime minister in 1940. He was a great leader. Above everything else, he had the ability to inspire the British people and to make them feel that they could win. This poster shows one of his most famous speeches.

◄ Winston Churchill often went out to meet workers and encourage them to keep going. In this photograph, a man is leaning forward to light his cigar.

► Laugh it off. This joke book shows how the British sense of humour was called upon to keep people's spirits up.

▲ Shops and businesses were bombed but often after a night of bombing, many shops with no windows put up a sign saying 'Business as Usual'. In this photograph there isn't even a shop left. The woman is selling goods to rescue workers from the pavement in front of the shop.

► The King and Queen stayed in Britain with both their daughters. They expected their daughters to grow up to play their part in the war. This photograph shows Princess Elizabeth (now Queen Elizabeth II) learning to change a wheel at an Auxiliary Territorial Service training centre.

# Entertainment

There was no television during the war but many people had a wireless (radio). Everyone wanted to listen to the news, particularly if a member of the family was fighting abroad or in the navy. People also liked to go to the cinema and forget the war for a while.

▼ This photograph was taken on 23 August 1940. The two men are BBC staff who are describing a fight between German and British planes, on the radio. A few minutes after this photograph was taken, these men were machine gunned by a German plane.

▲ Wireless sets were large and had to be plugged into an electricity socket. Usually the wireless was in the living room and the whole family gathered round to listen to it in the evening. As well as news bulletins and speeches from Winston Churchill, people enjoyed music and comedy shows.

◄ Bing Crosby was a very popular American film star and comedian. He can be seen broadcasting to the American and British troops for the BBC.

► Music and song became popular. Singers, such as Vera Lynn, gave people hope with songs like *'We'll Meet Again'*. Other songs, such as *'We're Gonna Hang Out the Washing on the Siegfried Line'*, were good for keeping up people's morale (The Siegfried Line was a line of German defences).

◄ Dancing was very popular. The American soldiers brought in a new dance called the jitterbug and jive. With so many men away fighting, women often danced together.

# Women in the War

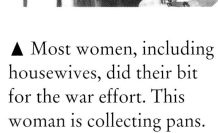

Many women worked hard as housewives. Their husbands were away and they ran the home. Many women went out to work as well. They worked in factories, or ran nurseries so other women could work. They built aeroplanes, trains, guns and tanks. They took over many jobs so that men could go and fight.

▼ Women working in a munitions factory. However good they were at their jobs, women got less pay than men for the same work.

▲ Most women, including housewives, did their bit for the war effort. This woman is collecting pans.

► A WVS (Women's Voluntary Service) canteen. About a million women did voluntary work for the WVS. They ran mobile canteens during the Blitz or they ran rest centres to take in bombed-out families. Other women drove ambulances, ran nurseries and helped with evacuees.

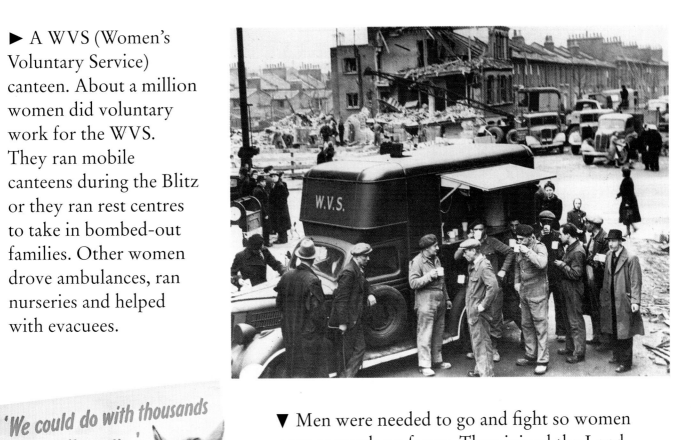

▼ Men were needed to go and fight so women went to work on farms. They joined the Land Army. They drove tractors and looked after animals. They planted potatoes and cut down trees.

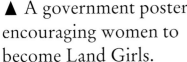

▲ A government poster encouraging women to become Land Girls.

# Women in Uniform

Women were called up but they were not allowed to fight. Many young women wanted to join the Army, Air Force or Navy. A very few women joined up but did not wear uniform because they belonged to the Special Operations Executive.

▲ Air ferry pilots. Women were not allowed to fly planes in battle but they did ferry new planes from the factories to the airfields.

▼ Other women joined the Women's Auxiliary Air Force (WAAF) and worked in the operation's rooms, or as radio operators, mechanics, nurses and cooks.

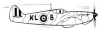 

◄ Barrage balloons were floated in the sky to stop enemy aircraft flying low. They were tethered to the ground. It took about sixteen women to get them up and down.

> ❝ I joined the ATS (Women's part of the army) and drove a three-ton truck. It was lovely living all that way from home. ❞
>
> **A ATS** VOLUNTEER

· A · T · S ·

◄ WRENS were the Women's Royal Naval Service. Wrens worked as river pilots, radio operators and drivers, working on ships and on land. This photograph shows a Wren demonstrating semaphore.

# POWs

Members of the armed forces who are taken prisoner during a war become prisoners of war (POWs). Britain did not win many battles for several years in the Second World War, so there were not many prisoners of war kept in Britain. In 1939 there were just two prisoner of war camps. However by1945, at the end of the war, there were six hundred camps.

▼ In 1939, thirty-four countries signed the Geneva Convention. This said that prisoners of war must be treated reasonably well. POWs could be made to do some work such as building roads and farm work.

◀ Many prisoners passed their spare time doing woodwork, such as making models.

◄ The northernmost prisoner of war camp was in Orkney, a group of islands off the north coast of Scotland. This was Camp 60 for Italian POWs. The Italians decided to make a chapel from one of their huts. Virtually everything had to be made from scrap and rubbish. They painted and decorated the building, inside and out to make a beautiful chapel.

The Red Cross visited the camps and made reports:

**Camp 197:** 5,270 men
**Breakfast:** a quarter of bread, margarine, ham, tea
**Dinner:** pork with potatoes
**Supper:** milk, soup, a fifth of bread

► This photograph shows two captured German spies dressed in American uniforms in 1944. Spies do not have the protection of the Geneva convention and these two were shot by American military police.

# The GIs

GI stands for General Issue. American soldiers were nicknamed GIs. America joined the war in 1941 and soon American airmen were coming to Britain to fly bombers against Germany. Later, thousands of GIs came over ready to invade Europe and defeat Germany.

▲ An American air gunner at an airbase in Britain in 1943. He is standing next to a Flying Fortress. The Americans set up their own airbases all over Britain and soon many thousands of American airmen were living here.

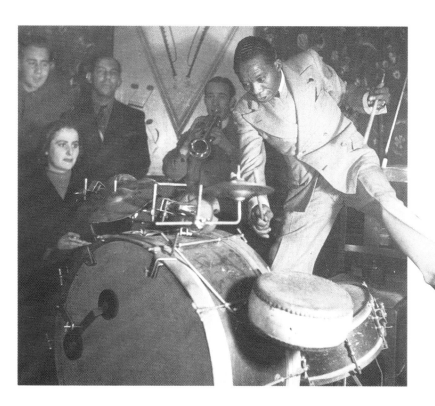

▲ The GIs brought new ideas, more food, new dances, music and fun to wartime Britain. This picture shows a drummer at an American GI club in 1943.

> 66 I met a girl at a dance and she asked me home to meet her family. When I went they laid on the best spread you'd ever seen. It was only when I got back to camp I learnt that this was the family's rations for a whole month. 99
>
> AN AMERICAN AIRMAN IN 1942

▼ The GIs had plenty of food and cigarettes. If an American soldier was asked to visit a British family, he was issued with tins of fruit, tins of meat, coffee, sugar and other things that were in short supply to take with him. The GIs also had plenty of luxuries such as sweets and silk stockings so children and women all liked the GIs.

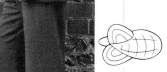

► By 1944 Britain and America were getting ready to invade Europe. Britain was full of GIs ready to cross into Europe. While they waited, many met up with British girls and decided to marry. They were called GI brides and many of them went to America with their new husbands when the war was over. The two GIs in this photograph married the two sisters leaning out of the window.

# Victory

By 1944, Britain and America felt strong enough to invade Europe and defeat Germany. They fought their way towards Germany. By the summer of 1945, the Allies had reached Germany. Adolf Hitler, the German leader committed suicide and Germany surrendered. At last the war in Europe was over.

> 66 How wonderful to be standing in Whitehall, in the shadow of the House of Commons, listening to That Voice which has steered us from our darkest hours to the daylight of deliverance. 99
>
> VERE HODGSON, WRITING ABOUT WINSTON CHURCHILL ON VE DAY; 8 MAY 1945

▼ British soldiers landing on the beaches in Normandy in France on 6th June 1944. This day was known as D-Day. 156,000 soldiers were landed on five beaches on the first day. The fighting was very fierce and many soldiers were killed. It took nearly a year for the British and Americans to reach Germany, but this was the beginning of the end of the war.

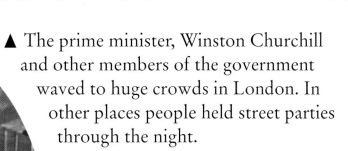

**News Chronicle**

# TODAY IS V DAY

### Churchill speaks at 3 p.m., the King at 9; Today and tomorrow are national holidays

They waited in Piccadilly Circus but had nothing to cheer

▲ VE Day stood for Victory in Europe. It took place on the 8th May 1945. The war had lasted six years and many lives had been lost. VE Day was a time of great celebrations for everyone in Britain.

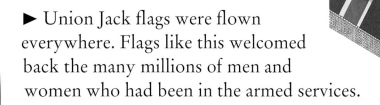

WELCOME BACK

▲ The prime minister, Winston Churchill and other members of the government waved to huge crowds in London. In other places people held street parties through the night.

► Union Jack flags were flown everywhere. Flags like this welcomed back the many millions of men and women who had been in the armed services.

◄ When the war was over the servicemen and women were no longer needed. They were demobilized or demobbed, and they handed in their uniform and were given a set of civilian clothes. Life was going to be very different.

# Time Line

**1938** Government started to issue gas masks.

*Sept 30* 30 million gas masks had been issued.

**1939**

*July* 20-year-old men called up to join the armed forces.

*Sept 1* Blackout first used.

*Sept 1* British evacuation of children, known as 'Operation Pied Piper', began.

*Sept 1* Germany invaded Poland.

*Sept 3* Britain and France declared war on Germany.

*Sept* Petrol put on ration.

**1940**

*Jan* Bacon, ham, sugar and butter put on ration.

*March* Meat rationing began.

*May 10* Germany invaded France. Winston Churchill became Prime Minister of Britain.

*May 14* The government asked for men to join the Local Defence Volunteers (later called the Home Guard).

*May 22* Government passed an Emergency Powers Law which put all citizens at the disposal of the Government.

*May 26–June 3* Evacuation of British and French soldiers from Dunkirk in France.

*May 27* Men aged 26 called up to join the armed forces.

*July 10* Battle of Britain began. German planes started attacking British airfields.

*Sept* End of Battle of Britain. Germans switched to attacking cities.

*Sept 7* First air raid on London, this was called Black Saturday.

*Nov 14* City of Coventry devastated.

*Nov 20* 300 German planes bombed Liverpool.

*Dec 29* Heaviest bombing raid on London started widespread fires.

**1941**

*Mar*      Night bombing raids on Glasgow left two-thirds of the population homeless.

*May*      Cheese and jam rationed.

*May*      The Blitz ended.

*June*     Clothes rationed.

*July 18*  National Fire Service formed to take over from local service.

*Dec*      All women between 18 and 50 could be called on to do some war work.

*Dec*      Tinned food rationed.

**1942**

*Feb 4*    Beaverbrook appointed Minister of Production because more and more goods needed to be made for the war.

*Feb*      Soap rationed.

*April 23* Bombing raids on beautiful old cities began.

*July*     Petrol unavailable except for essential services such as fire engines and doctors.

*Oct*      Women up to 45 had to do war work unless their children were under 14.

*Dec 2*    Beveridge report published to plan for a better Britain after the war.

**1943**

*July 4*   Call-up of women up to the age of 50.

**1944**

*June 6*   D-Day landings in France.

*June 13*  The first VI unmanned bombs landed in Britain.

*Sept 8*   The first V2 unmanned bombs landed in Britain.

*Dec 3*    The Home Guard was disbanded.

**1945**

*Mar 27*   The last V2 landed in Britain.

*May 8*    The Allies captured Berlin and declared Victory in Europe.

*April 6*  Atom bombs dropped on Hiroshima and Nagasaki.

*Aug 15*   Japan surrendered.

# Glossary

**Air raid siren** Machine that makes a loud noise to warn people of possible air raids.

**Allotment** An area of land for growing food.

**Battledress** Soldier's trousers and jacket for fighting in.

**Bazaar** A sale of goods usually to raise money.

**Blitzrieg** A very fast attack.

**Bomb disposal** To safely get rid of unexploded bombs.

**Bomb site** Empty space where a bomb had fallen.

**Civilian clothes** You own everyday clothes which are not a uniform.

**Comradeship** Friendship.

**Conflict** A fight.

**Code** A secret language used to send top secret information.

**Demobbed** Leaving the armed forces.

**Demolished** To completely destroy something, usually a building.

**Devastated** To ruin something.

**Disbanded** The breaking up of a group of people who no longer work together.

**Drill** To practise the same thing over and over again.

**Evacuation** Emptying something or leaving somewhere.

**Fighter plane** A fast aeroplane with guns to shoot down enemy aeroplanes.

**Gas mask** A cover for the nose and mouth to filter out poisonous gas.

**Geneva Convention** An international agreement to look after the sick and injured, and prisoners of war, during wartime.

**Invasion** The forceful entry into another country or somebody else's land.

**Knapsack** A bag to carry on the back.

**Morale** The way you feel – your morale could be high or low.

**Munitions factory** A factory where shells and bullet were made.

**Parachutist** A soldier parachutist.

**Phoney war** The time from September 1939 to May 1940 when Britain was at war but nothing much happened.

**Propaganda** Information which is intended to make people think in a certain way.

**Pulped down** A process where used paper is broken down to make recycled paper.

**Radar** Transmitting a wave that bounced off objects such as ships and aeroplanes so revealing how near or far away they were.

**Rally** A meeting of people to support something or someone that they believe in.

**Residential** An area or place where people live.

**Salvage** To use something, such as waste paper and scrap metal, again and make something new.

**Spy** Someone who finds out information and gives it to the enemy.

**Surrendered** To give yourself up to your enemy.

**Timetable** A list of events, or a list of arrivals and departures of transport, with the times they will happen.

**Underground** The tunnels in London for underground trains are often just called the Underground.

**Voluntary worker** Someone who works without getting paid.

**Wary** Be careful and watch out for danger.

**Wireless** A radio.

# Further Information

## Books to read
### Non-fiction

*A Day in the Life of a World War II Evacuee* by Alan Childs (Wayland, 1999)

*Britain in World War II – The Blitz* by Patricia Kendell (Wayland, 1998)

*Daily Life in a Wartime House* by Laura Wilson (Heinemann, 1997))

*The History Detective Investigates Britain at War* (Four book series including: *Evacuation, Women's War, Air Raids, Rationing)* by Martin Parsons (Wayland, 1999)

*Home in the Blitz* by Marilyn Tolhurst (A&C Black, 1996)

*The Home Front* (Six book series including:*The Blitz, Evacuation, Prisoners of War, Propaganda, Rationing, Women's War)* by Fiona Reynoldson (Wayland, 1990)

*Horrible Histories: The Blitzed Brits* by Terry Deary (Scholastic, 1996)

*Reputations in History: Winston Churchill. The Man who Saved the World?* by Josh Brooman (Longman, 1999)

*Scotland and the Second World War* by Simon Wood (Hodder & Stoughton, 1997))

*Scotland in World War II* by Richard Dargie (Wayland, 1997)

*Wartime Cookbook* by Brian Moses (Wayland, 1995)

*What Families Were Like: Second World War* by Fiona Reynoldson (Wayland, 1998)

*When I was Young, World War II* by Neil Thompson (Franklin Watts, 1993)

## Fiction

*Carrie's War* by Nina Bawden (Penquin, 1974)

*Goodnight Mr Tom* by Michelle Magorian (Penquin, 1983)

*Harry's Battle of Britain* by Andrew Donkin (Macdonald Young, 1999)

*Lizzy's War* by Elizabeth Beresford (Macdonald Young, 1994)

## Places to visit
**Cabinet War Rooms, London**
Churchill's secret underground headquarters.
Tel: 0891 600 140

**Duxford Airfield, Cambridgeshire**
A former RAF fighter airfield and US base.
Tel: 01223 835 000

**HMS Belfast, London**
The last surviving Royal Navy big gun ship is now a floating naval museum
Tel: 0171 407 6434

**Imperial War Museum, London**
Displays covering the First and Second World Wars and the 'Blitz Experience'.
Tel: 0171 416 5000

**Kent Battle of Britain Museum, Hawkinge, near Folkstone, Kent**
Many artefacts from daily life, anything from gas masks to ration cards.
Tel: 01303 893 140

**The Italian Chapel, Orkney, Scotland**
The chapel built by Italian POWs is well worth a visit if on holiday in Orkney.

# Index

Numbers in **bold** refer to pictures as well as text.